Harmonic Dressage

PART 2

Techniques of Harmonic Dressage and the Training Pyramid

Gail Hoff, PhD

First Published in the United States of America in 2022 by Los Alamos Dressage Center, 461 Buckboard Lane, Ojai, CA 93023

COPYRIGHT © 2021 by Gail Hoff
All rights Reserved Including the right of reproduction, in whole or in part in any form by any means.

ISBN: 978-1-7353111-2-8

Library of Congress Control Number: 2022903975

Illustrations, Book Design and Cover by Daniel Marhuenda Donadeu

Back Cover Photo: Jan Eisner

Table of Contents

Acknowledgements — 7

Introduction — 10

What is the Training Pyramid — 13
    Interaction of Elements on the
    Training Pyramid — 18

The Elements of the Training Pyramid — 22
    <u>Element 1</u> – Rhythm, Regularity
    and Tempo of Gaits — 22
        The Gaits — 22
        Rhythm, Regularity
        and Tempo — 23
        Walk Paces — 25
        Trot Paces — 27
        Canter Paces — 31
        Deviations from the Purity
        of the Gaits — 35
        Improving the Gaits — 38

    <u>Element 2</u> – Relaxation and
    Suppleness — 41
        Relaxation — 41
        Relaxation and Suppleness — 42
        Suppleness — 42
        Characteristics of Relaxation
        and Suppleness — 43

Traits of Good Relaxation and Suppleness	**44**
Creating Mental Relaxation	**44**
Creating Muscular Relaxation (Suppling)	**46**
The Anatomy of Bending	**47**
Exercises to Promote Relaxation and Suppleness	**53**
Element 3 – Contact and Connection	**69**
Creating and Assessing Contact and Connection	**70**
Framing – Getting on the Aids	**72**
Element 4 – Impulsion	**79**
Traits of Good Impulsion	**82**
Element 5 – Straightness	**85**
Lateral Exercises to Improve Straightness	**86**
Specifics of Shoulder-In	**88**
Lateral Movements to Improve Straightness	**90**
Specifics of Travers (Haunches-In)	**93**
Half-Pass = Tavers on a Diagonal Line	**94**
Element 6 – Collection	**96**
Collection and the Training Pyramid	**97**

The Movements and their Purpose **100**
    Halt **100**
    Half-Halt **100**
    Rein Back **101**
    Transitions **101**
    Changes of Direction **102**
    Leg-Yield **103**
    Turn on the Forehand **103**
    Shoulder-In and Shoulder-Fore **104**
    Travers, Renvers and Half-Pass **105**
    Pirouette and Turn on the Haunches **107**
    Piaffe **108**
    Passage **109**

Putting it All Together **110**

Index **113**

Acknowledgements

My deepest gratitude goes to all the horses I have trained, the students I have taught and who have taught me as well, the many excellent instructors and clinicians I was fortunate enough to learn from, and my training and experience as a dressage judge for more than 40 years.

I am especially grateful to my editor, Barbara Christopher, who not only offered many excellent suggestions, but who also has a very keen eye. She has been both inspiring and of immeasurable assistance.

A special thanks to Wally Shaker, Joyce Swanson, and Wendy Wergeles for reviewing this book. Wally, a longtime friend, is a horse trainer and instructor in Germany. He also runs a sales barn for both jumpers and dressage horses near Hamburg, Germany. His experience and knowledge of the classic German Training Pyramid served as a valuable check point for this book. Joyce is a "R" western dressage judge and a founding member of the Western Dressage Association in America (WDAA). She orchestrated writing the rules and the tests for western dressage competitions and has helped to organize seminars to train western dressage judges. Her valuable insights are very appreciated. Wendy is an Advanced /4★ level 3-day Event Rider, USEF "R" eventing judge and an "S" technical delegate who graciously reviewed and commented on this book with an eye especially as to how it relates to horses used for eventing. Her multifaceted perspective of training and judging horses made her an extremely appreciated reviewer.

A huge thank you to Ann James, former student, FEI rider, and dressage trainer who always very generously shares her opinions and insights with me. She was very helpful, especially when organizing and clarifying topics in the earlier stages of the manuscript.

To my former students, Christian Simonsen and Katarina Antens-Miller, I am deeply indebted for their undying support and multitude of photos and videos. Their contributions of so many media allowed me to find and select images otherwise difficult to find. Katarina Antens-Miller, a USDF Gold Medalist, is a native of Sweden who trains and rides her own Swedish Warmbloods. Christian was about ten years old when he began learning dressage from me and, as I write this book, Christian is currently National Champion FEI Young Rider who stands third place in the world on the FEI Young Riders list with his Danish

Warmblood, Zeaball Diawind.

To the Olympic riders, Adrienne Lyle and Sabine Schut-Kery, I am deeply indebted for sharing photos representing not only the excellent horses they ride but also their skill as top riders and trainers.

Huge thanks go to several other contributors of valuable images. Among them are, in alphabetical order: Sarah Borray, Alberto Conde, Judi Devore, Kamila Dupont, Jorge Gabriel, Sarah Graham, Efrain Guzman, Karin Harkin, Ava Johnson, Lorraine Kainuma, Glen Thompson, Tami Thompson, and Courtney Welch. Without the support of everyone, this book would not have been possible.

Introduction

Learning to train a horse is truly the journey of a lifetime. Hubert Rohrer, a good friend of mine with a good sense of humor, was a dressage trainer and judge trained at the Spanish Riding School in Vienna. He once said to me that learning to train a horse first requires that you learn to sit correctly and ride a well-trained horse. Secondly, you need to learn how to train a horse. Thirdly, when you finally learn how to train a horse correctly, you are probably too old to do it anymore.

It is true that dressage training is a never-ending journey. Each horse can teach us something and yet, the underlying principles for training horses as put forth by the Training Pyramid or training-scale, can be applied to any horse. Dressage simply means training and its principles, as laid out by the Training Pyramid, applies to any horse in any discipline. How the principles are applied, and to what extent each is emphasized, can, however, vary from horse to horse as well as from discipline to discipline. Never-the-less, the principles remain constant.

In this book, it is my intent to explore each of the principles or elements of the Training Pyramid in detail and try to show how they work together both as a hierarchy as well as an interactive scale. Truly understanding these concepts can not only serve as a guide to trainers wishing to train horses up the levels in dressage but also to trainers simply wishing to make their horses easier to ride in whatever discipline they might choose.

Harmonic Dressage®, a system of training both horse and rider, is based totally upon the classic German Training Pyramid with particular emphasis placed upon the use of the back of the horse.

The back of the horse is like a bridge that connects the forequarters to the hindquarters. When it is strong and supple, the horse can easily carry the weight of the rider and move with elasticity and freedom. When it is hollowed or stiff, the horse becomes prone to unsoundness and the ability to move with elasticity and freedom also suffers.

Truly understanding the hierarchy of the Training Pyramid as well as how all of the elements are interconnected offers trainers the opportunity to develop a clear system of training as well as a path to understanding and solving problems as they might arise.

In this book, each element on the Training Pyramid/scale will be examined and some techniques commonly used to improve each of them will be set forth. In addition, the interaction of all of the elements will be explored as they all profoundly affect each other. When a rider truly understands the Training Pyramid and how the elements interact, then the training of the horse can progress in a logical and systematic manner because a horse is always prepared in advance, both mentally and physically, to be able to perform more difficult tasks. Just as a composer of music uses each note when composing music, it is the interaction of the notes that creates the music. This is also true when using the Training Pyramid to train a horse. All of the elements of the Training Pyramid interact and work together to progress the training of the horse. When a trainer truly understands the Training Pyramid, he/she will also know the best ways to address difficulties during training in order to find a good solution.

Using the Training Pyramid to train a horse well requires that the rider understands the theory well. In addition, the rider must learn to be seated correctly and know how and when to apply the aids correctly. *Harmonic Dressage, Part 1, Optimizing Your Seat and Use of the Aids* explores that subject in detail, and it is advisable for anyone wishing to do dressage to review Part 1.

What Is the Training Pyramid?

The classic Training Pyramid is a schematic portraying a rational system of training horses. It is described in *The Principles of Riding* (Official Instruction Handbook of the German National Equestrian Federation) and is a system for training horses to become more supple, elastic, balanced, and stronger. It promotes both lateral (side to side) and longitudinal (back to front) flexibility in a horse. Thus, as the training of a horse progresses, the horse will become capable of more engagement of the hindquarters. This, in turn, enables the horse to carry more weight behind, which then creates a relative lifting and lightness of the forehand.

The Training Pyramid is composed of six elements. Each element builds upon the foundation of the former element such that a diagram of it looks like a pyramid (Fig. 1). Consequently, it has become known both as the Training Pyramid. It is important to truly understand why there is a hierarchy creating the Training Pyramid. It is equally important to truly understand the intricate interaction of all of the elements. Using the Training Pyramid to train a horse implies that each of the elements should be addressed in a specific order.

The Training Pyramid

Fig. 1
Training Pyramid (German word in red under English translation)

Collection *Versammlung*	Increased Engagement, Lightness of forehand, Self-Carriage	
Straightness *Geraderichtung*	Improved Alignment and Balance	
Impulsion *Schwung*	Increased Energy and Thrust	
Connection or Contact *Anlehnung*	Acceptance of the Bit through Acceptance of the Aids	
Suppleness *Losgelassenheit*	Elasticity and Relaxation	
Rhythm and Regularity *Takt*	With Energy and Tempo	

Why the Training Pyramid is also Called the Training Scale or Training Wheel

Although the shape of the Training Pyramid suggests a chronological mastery of skills, it does not mean that the first element at the bottom of the pyramid should be perfected before one proceeds to the next higher element. All of the elements are interactive and work together in harmony with each other (Fig. 2). The pyramid depicts a hierarchy between the elements which is fundamental to understanding their interaction. The first three elements: 1) rhythm and regularity 2) suppleness and relaxation 3) connection and contact, are the foundation of training a horse. These three elements must be present in any horse at any level of training. The higher three elements: 4) impulsion 5) straightness 6) collection, are dependent upon the first three elements. Without the first three elements interacting properly, the higher three elements cannot be well executed. Likewise, each element builds upon the lower element. For instance, rhythm and regularity need to be maintained in order to create suppleness. These first two elements, when achieved, will then pave the pathway to create a suppled and relaxed connection or framing over the back of the horse. Impulsion, not just speed, is not possible without first creating suppleness and a good connection. Impulsion then sets the stage for more straightness which then creates harmonious and relaxed collection.

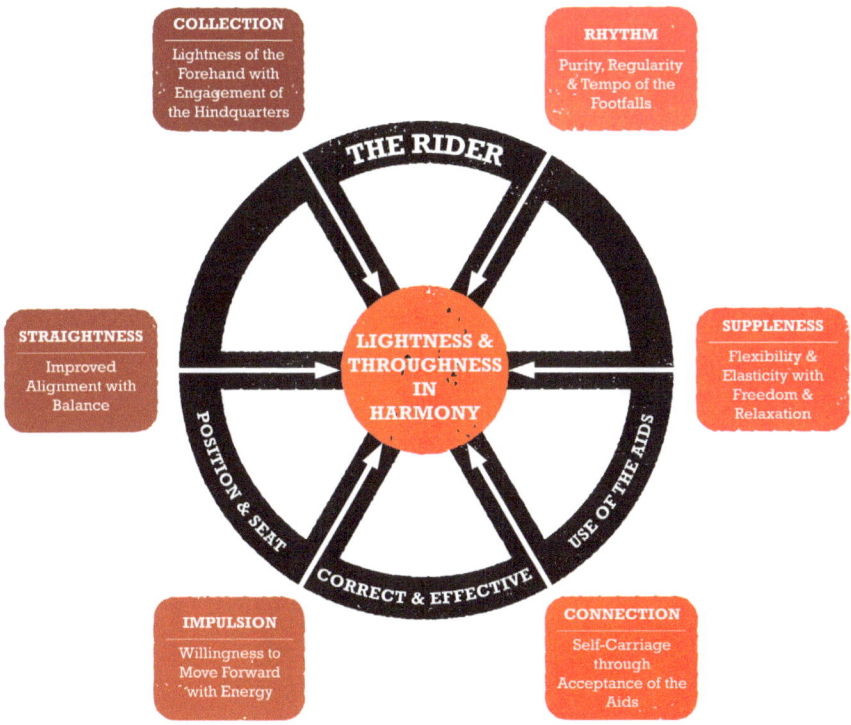

Fig. 2 The Training Wheel
This image has the permission of the Western Dressage Association of America

Interaction of Elements on the Training Pyramid

Understanding the principles of the Training Pyramid is key to understanding the language of the horse.

Because of the interaction of the elements on the Training Pyramid, the rider should be aware of the element lowest on the pyramid that is difficult for the horse at that time. That element will be the weakest link and should be addressed first and foremost. However, to address a particular element, other elements on the Training Pyramid will need to be applied because they are interactive and work in harmony with each other. By addressing and correcting the lowest element on the scale, the rider can then move to the next lowest element and continue in that fashion. Thus, the Training Pyramid serves as a guide to a rational and logical way to train a horse.

Using the Elements as a Guide

Issue: Imagine that a horse has been examined by a veterinarian and found to be sound. It is, however, showing periodic irregularity at the trot and is reluctant to move forward.

Solution: Since rhythm and regularity are the lowest elements on the Training Pyramid and impulsion is higher up on it, the rider first needs to determine what is causing the irregularity before lack of desire to move forward (impulsion) is addressed.

If a rider focuses first upon the roundness and suppleness of the back of the horse and explores possible reasons for hollowness or stiffness, the rider can then probably determine what is creating the hollowness or stiffness. The most common reason for irregularity is that the back of the horse is hollow and/or stiff. The back of a horse could be likened to a bridge. When the back is rounded and supple, it is relaxed and strong like a bridge. When the back is hollowed or stiff, it is weak like a broken bridge. It is not possible to create impulsion by pushing against a stiff or hollowed back (broken bridge.) Pushing against it simply creates more stiffness and weakness. Impulsion is dependent upon the first three elements of the Training Pyramid, which create a supple connection over the back of the horse and allow the horse to move forward in a relaxed manner.

Tension over the back of the horse is often created by the rider's inability to establish a strong and supple connection over the back of the horse. This is often a result of a rider taking too much contact with the mouth of the horse so that the horse's head is being held up and/or the neck is being shortened by the rider's hands. This, in turn, will stiffen the back of the horse and prevent it from rounding and relaxing its back.

If a rider relaxes his/her arms more and allows the horse to lower and lengthen its neck some, the rider will eventually feel where the back of the horse is relaxed and swinging and can then determine whether or not the rhythm and regularity of the gait has improved. If regularity has improved because the back has become more supple, then the rider can supple the horse further with various exercises in order to create a better connection. When a better connection is achieved, it is then possible to drive the horse more forward to create a stronger connection over the back of the horse. Rhythm and regularity reflect the interaction of all of the other elements of the Training Pyramid. When a sound horse is suppled, connected over its back, and moving forward, it will begin to straighten itself. Straightness will then produce collection.

Another common reason that stiffness is created over the back of the horse is due to a rider trying to ride the horse too straight before it is sufficiently laterally flexible. Remember that suppleness is the second element on the Training Pyramid and straightness is the fifth.

Since straightness is near the top of the pyramid (**Element 5**) and suppling of the horse is lower on the Training Pyramid (**Element 2**) than contact/connection (**Element 3**) this information should help the rider to know that he/she needs to work with suppling exercises (**Element 2**) that include lateral flexibility and promote self-carriage. In order to do suppling exercises, the rider must also be able to establish a good connection (**Element 3**) over the back of the horse by activating the hind legs of the horse and sending it forward with impulsion

(**Element 4**) into a receiving hand so that the horse can then lift and round its back. Once the regularity of the trot (**Element 1**) is achieved through the combined interaction of **Elements 2 and 3** (suppling and connection,) increasing impulsion (**Element 4**) will then be possible and will lead to more straightness (**Element 5**) which creates collection (**Element 6**).

With rhythm and regularity (**Element 1**) restored, a rider can then begin work with suppling exercises (**Element 2**).
Suppling exercises require a rider to establish an elastic contact and connection (**Element 3**).

Horses, like people, have different strengths and weaknesses. Consequently, how a rider should apply the aids varies somewhat according to the needs of that particular horse at that particular moment.

The Elements of the Training Pyramid

1. Rythm, Regularity and Tempo of Gaits *(Takt)*

The Gaits

At the base of the Training Pyramid lie the purity (clear four beat walk, two beat trot, three beat canter) and tempo of all three gaits. Without these prerequisites in place, no further good training is possible. The rhythm and regularity of the gaits reflect not only the natural gaits of the horse but also all of the other elements of the Training Pyramid and how well they are working in harmony. They also reflect the overall balance and throughness (acceptance of the aids of the rider without resistance) of the horse.

Each gait has its own rhythm and regularity. The horse should be able to do walk, trot, and canter in the correct rhythm with an energetic and clearly regular tempo. In German, the combination of rhythm, energy, regularity and tempo is called *takt* but there is no equivalent English word for it. Consequently, the use of the words, rhythm and regularity, will also imply energetic tempo. (Fig. 3)

There are three gaits natural to all horses except gaited horses (horses that have been bred to do a four-beat pace instead of a two-beat trot, such as the Tennessee Walking horse). Within each of the three gaits (walk, trot, and canter) there are variations which are referred to as paces.

The individual paces (i.e.: collected, medium, and extended) within each gait are simply points along a continuum. In other words, the rhythm, regularity, and tempo remain constant, but the length and height of the stride vary according to the pace being performed.

Rhythm, Regularity and Tempo

- **Rhythm**
    - Walk = 4 beats (each hoof lands separately)
    - Trot = 2 beats (diagonal pairs of legs land together)
    - Canter = 3 beats (1 diagonal pair lands together followed by 2 individual steps which are separated by a moment of suspension)

- **Regularity**
    - Evenness in length of steps
    - Levelness in height of steps
    - Leg pairs are symmetrical in height and length

- **Tempo**
    - Rate of repetition of strides

Fig. 3

Rhythm is the <u>recurring characteristic sequence</u> and timing of footfalls and phases of a gait.

Regularity refers to the <u>purity</u> of the gait. At the walk and trot, regularity denotes symmetry in terms of

    a) evenness of the length of the steps (hind legs reach under the horse as much as the forelimbs of the horse extend from the shoulders.

    b) levelness of the height of the steps (left and right hind legs or left and right forelegs should lift equally.)

    c) and equality of the time interval between the steps

Tempo is the <u>rate of repetition</u> of the rhythm. Tempo is measured by counting the number of times per minute that one of the hooves touches down (indicating completion of one full stride.) Tempo can be measured with a metronome.

Walk Paces

A clear, four-beat marching rhythm as well as a steady tempo and relaxed back should be maintained between all variations of the walk. There are four walk paces: free, extended, medium, and collected walks. Fig. 4 shows a comparison of the walk paces and each one is discussed in Figs. 5-8.

Free Walk

Photo Courtesy of Ava Johnson

Medium Walk

Photo Courtesy of Ava Johnson

Extended Walk

Photo Courtesy of Christian Simonson

Collected Walk

Photo Courtesy of Christian Simonson

Fig. 4 Comparison of Walk Paces

Photo Courtesy of Ava Johnson

Fig. 5 Free Walk

In the free walk (Fig. 5), the horse stretches its neck down and out with complete freedom on a loose rein. The stride becomes as ground covering as possible, and the hind legs should track up as much as forelegs reach forward from the shoulder. The hind feet should step several inches in front of the hoofprints of the front feet. The back of the horse should swing and be elastic with each step.

Photo Courtesy of Christian Simonson

Fig. 6 Extended Walk

The extended walk (Fig. 6) is similar to the free walk in that the horse covers as much ground per stride as possible. The hind feet touch the ground clearly in front of the hoof prints of the fore feet. However, in the extended walk, the horse maintains a light contact with the bit. The neck should remain long and stretch down and out as the horse seeks contact with the bit, but the reins do not become loose.

Photo Courtesy of Ava Johnson

Fig. 7 Medium Walk

The medium walk (Fig. 7) is similar to the natural walk of the horse. Although the horse remains "on the bit," the head and neck of the horse show natural movement. The medium walk is not as ground covering as the free or extended walk, but the hind feet step clearly in front (ideally, about 2 hoof lengths) of the hoofprints of the front feet.

Photo Courtesy of Christian Simonson

Fig. 8 Collected Walk

In the collected walk (Fig. 8), the strides become shorter and higher than at other paces of the walk because all joints bend more markedly. The collected walk should show animation and not be slower than the other walk paces. The horse remains in self-carriage and "on the bit" with its neck raised and the nose near the vertical due to more engagement of the hindquarters.

Trot Paces

The trot has five paces which are related to the length of stride. These paces are collected, working, lengthening of stride, medium, and extended. A comparison of the trot paces is shown in Fig. 9 and each one discussed in Figs. 10 – 14. In all the paces, the canon bone of the hind leg should be parallel to the forearm of the diagonal foreleg (Fig. 21). The ability of a horse to lengthen its stride depends upon its conformation, strength, and the degree of training.

Extended Trot

Photo Courtesy of Sabine Schut-Kery and Anne Womble, owner of Sanceo

Medium Trot

Jan Eisner Photo Courtesy of Katerina Antens - Miller

Lengthening of Stride

Jan Eisner Photo Courtesy of Katerina Antens - Miller

Working Trot

Jan Eisner Photo Courtesy of Katerina Antens - Miller

Collected Trot

Susan Stickle Photo Courtesy of Christian Simonson

Fig. 9 Comparison of Trot Paces

Photo Courtesy of Sabine Schut-Kery and Anne Womble, owner of Sanceo

Fig. 10 Extended Trot

In the <u>extended trot</u> (Fig. 10), the horse covers as much ground as possible. Without increasing speed, the steps are lengthened as much as possible as a result of great impulsion from the hindquarters. The fore feet should touch the ground on the spot towards which they are pointing. (The front hooves should not flip up.) The movement of the fore and hind legs should reach equally forward in the moment of extension. The horse should remain straight without spreading the hindlegs.

Jsn Eisner Photo Courtesy of Katerina Antens - Miller

Fig. 11 Medium Trot

<u>Medium trot</u> (Fig. 11) is similar to the extended trot except that the length of the steps is slightly less. Due to increased impulsion from the hindquarters, the horse goes forward without increasing speed.

Susan Stickle Photo Courtesy of Christian Simonson

Fig. 12 Collected Trot

In the <u>collected trot</u> (Fig. 12), the horse, remaining "on the bit," moves forward with the neck raised and arched as it comes into complete self-carriage. The hocks should be well-engaged and flexed. Energetic impulsion should be maintained to enable the shoulders to move with greater freedom. Although the horse's steps are shorter than in the other trots, elasticity, cadence, and tempo are not decreased.

Jan Eisner Photo
Courtesy of Katerina Antens - Miller

Fig. 13 Lengthen Stride in Trot

<u>Lengthening of stride</u> (Fig. 13) is a variation between the working and medium trot. The steps are clearly lengthened but, because the horse's training is not developed enough to create sufficient impulsion and collection, the horse remains in a more horizonal balance than in medium trot.

Jan Eisner Photo
Courtesy of Katerina Antens - Miller

Fig. 14 Working Trot

The <u>working trot</u> (Fig. 14) is a pace between the collected and the medium trot. It is similar to the natural trot of a horse that is not yet developed enough for collected movements. The horse shows proper balance and, remaining "on the bit," goes forward with even, elastic steps generated by well flexed and active hocks.

Canter Paces

The canter, like the trot, has five paces that are related to the length of stride. These canter paces are collected, working, lengthening of stride, medium, and extended. A comparison of them is shown in Fig. 15, and each one discussed in Figs. 16 – 20.

All canter paces should be 3 beat or appear as 3 beats. They may vary in beats per minute according to the ideal tempo for that particular pace.

Extended Canter
Photo Courtesy of Kamila Dupont

Medium Canter
Jsn Eisner Photo Courtesy of Katerina Antens - Miller

Lengthening of Stride
Aston Kingsley Photo Courtesy of Tami Thompson

Working Canter
Aston Kingsley Photo Courtesy of Tami Thompson

Collected Canter
Photo Courtesy of Christian Simonson

Fig. 15 Comparison of Canter Paces

Photo Courtesy of Kamila Dupont

Fig. 16
Extended Canter

In the <u>extended canter</u> (Fig. 16), the horse covers as much ground as possible. Without increasing speed, the strides are lengthened to the utmost as a result of engagement and great impulsion from the hindquarters.

*Jan Eisner Photo
Courtesy of Katerina Antens - Miller*

Fig. 17
Medium Canter

The <u>medium canter</u> (Fig. 17) is a pace between the working and the extended canter. Without rushing, the horse goes forward with clearly lengthened strides due to engagement and impulsion from the hindquarters. The strides should be balanced and unconstrained.

Photo Courtesy of Christian Simonson

Fig. 18
Collected Canter

In the <u>collected canter</u> (Fig. 18), the horse, remaining "on the bit," moves forward with the neck raised and arched due to increased engagement of the hind quarters and active, flexing hocks that maintain an energetic impulsion. This enables the shoulders to move with greater freedom, so the horse demonstrates self-carriage and an uphill balance. The horse's strides are shorter than in the other canters, but without losing elasticity and cadence.

*Aston Kingsley Photo
Courtesy of Tami Thompson*

Fig. 19 Lengthen Stride in Canter

Lengthening of stride in the canter (Fig. 19) is a variation between the working and medium canter in which a horse's training is not developed enough for medium canter. The steps are clearly lengthened but, because the horse's training is not developed enough to create sufficient impulsion, the horse remains in a more horizonal balance than in medium canter.

*Aston Kingsley Photo
Courtesy of Tami Thompson*

Fig. 20 Working Canter

The working canter (Fig. 20) is similar to the natural canter of the horse. It is a pace between the collected and the medium canter, in which a horse's training is not yet developed enough and ready for collected movements. The horse, while remaining "on the bit," and goes forward with even, light and active strides and good separation of the hind legs.

Deviations from the Purity of the Gaits

Assuming that a horse's limbs are sound, when deviations in the gaits occur while riding, they should become a signal to the rider that the back of the horse is probably not as supple as it should be. An empathetic rider will then try to determine the reason why there is a deviation. Physical issues, correctly fitted tack, as well as training methodology can all play a part in creating deviations within the gait(s).

The most common deviations within the gaits are:

1. The walk most commonly <u>loses a clear four-beat rhythm</u> where the timing between footfalls is equal. The walk commonly deteriorates into a lateral or pacing walk where the hind leg and foreleg on the same side move in unison or have a tendency to move in unison. Since there is no impulsion (moment of suspension) in the walk, this gait is very susceptible to impurities.

2. The trot <u>does not clearly show diagonal pairs</u> (Figs. 21 and 22) where the canon bone of the hind leg is parallel to the forearm of the diagonal foreleg. This is sometimes a result of the conformation of the horse but can also be created by stiffness or hollowness over the back of the horse.

Fig. 21 Trot with Diagonal Pairs

Fig. 22 Disunited Trot Lacking Diagonal Pairs

3 The canter becomes lateral or broken into a four-beat gait. There should be good separation of the hind legs in the canter. The outside hind leg, which initiates the canter, should step well under the body of the horse so that it can raise the forehand of the horse and allow for good separation of the hind legs.

In a lateral canter the hind leg and foreleg on the same side land almost in unison and the canter is almost two-beat rather than three-beat (Fig. 23). A four-beat canter (Fig. 24) usually refers to a horse which is moving very slowly and is on the forehand. Each foot lands at a different time. Since the outside hind leg fails to propel the horse enough to sufficiently lift the forehand, the moment of suspension and clear three beat, which are characteristic of the canter, are lost. An observer will be able to notice the diagonal dissociation and will also be able to hear the four beats.

Although an inactive and clearly four-beat canter is undesirable, some horses do display active four-beat canters in the collected canter. Four beat canters are also apparent in the canter pirouette or the gallop. The main difference is that in active four-beat canters, the four beats are not perceptible to the naked eye because the diagonal pair touch the ground almost simultaneously (Fig. 25).

Fig. 23 Lateral Canter
The hind leg and foreleg on the same side land almost in unison

Fig. 24 Four-Beat Canter on Forehand
Each foot lands at a different time and perceptible to the naked eye

Fig. 25 Active Four-Beat Canter Pirouette
Each foot lands at a different time but imperceptible to naked eye

Improving the Gaits

In all the gaits, contact and connection (Element 3) need to be correctly established to allow the horse to move freely. Riders need to create the horse's self-carriage and must not block the movement of the horse by keeping their arms tense and applying undue pressure on the lower jaw of the horse. Strong arms encourage the horse to lean against the hands of the rider because the neck of the horse is shortened, and the horse is not allowed to carry its own head. This is uncomfortable for the horse and, in an effort to gain better balance and self-carriage, the horse will tighten its neck muscles, especially the lower neck muscles and brace against the rider's hands. In turn, the back of the horse is also tensed and dropped or hollowed under the seat of the rider. When the back of the horse is tight and no longer rounded, it becomes weaker and cannot serve effectively as a strong bridge between the hindquarters and forehand of the horse. All this tension and stiffness lead to deterioration of the gaits. For more details on how to avoid creating this problem, refer to *Harmonic Dressage, Part 1, Optimizing Your Seat and Use of the Aids,* pages 30-39.

Exercises to Improve Rhythm, Regularity and Tempo (Element 1)

Lateral and longitudinal work address suppling and relaxation (Element 2).
Horses bend both laterally (side to side) and longitudinally (poll to tail). Exercises such as using the unilateral aids followed by straightening with the diagonal aids, bending lines, turn on the forehand and leg-yields all help the horse to become more laterally supple.

Suppling a horse <u>first laterally and then framing and straightening longitudinally</u> will help a horse to become more round over its topline and engage the hindquarters without becoming stiff. This will then allow the horse to find good balance and take even contact with the hands of the rider on both sides of its mouth. Bending, first to the inside followed by framing with the outside aids, will begin to straighten a horse. Framing, together with additional impulsion, will then create straightness. Straightness will strengthen the role of the back as a bridge between the hind quarters and the forehand and produce longitudinal bend due to engagement of the hindquarters. All of these components will improve the quality and elasticity of the gaits. However, if a rider tries to create straightness in the horse before first suppling it laterally, especially through the lumbosacral area by having the horse cross its hind legs, most horses will stiffen their backs and joints and the gaits will deteriorate.

Cavaletti

In addition to training exercises, cavaletti work can also be very useful to:

1 Help the walk to become a clear four-beat gait.

2 Help the trot and canter to develop more balance, expression, collection, or extension.

3 Help to keep the horse's mind focused upon its job and to actively think about what it is doing.

Since all of the elements of the Training Pyramid are interactive, all of the elements will become more pronounced as a horse progresses in its training. The gaits will reflect correct training by becoming more elastic, elevated, and cadenced.

2. Relaxation and Suppleness
(Lossgelassenheit)

Relaxation

For horses to learn and perform well, they need to be relaxed both mentally and physically (Fig. 26). Mental relaxation refers to calmness without anxiety or nervousness. In other words, the horse is at ease, co-operative and unagitated. Physical relaxation refers to the muscular relaxation needed to create supple and fluid movement as well as freedom in the range of motion of joints. Flexibility and pliability together with freedom of motion are the hallmarks of physical relaxation.

Relaxation and Suppleness

- **Mental Relaxation**
  - Calmness without anxiety or nervousness
  - At ease & cooperative

- **Physical = Muscular Relaxation**
  - Needed to create fluid movement
  - Needed for full range of motion of joints, flexibility and pliability

Fig. 26

Suppleness

The back and trunk of the horse play a coordinating role between the hind quarters and forehand. When an aid is applied by a rider to the rib cage of the horse, it is transmitted throughout the body and limbs of the horse. However, if a horse is either tense or too relaxed, the back muscles cannot fulfill their coordinating role. Teaching the horse to use its back muscles correctly as well as conditioning to promote mental relaxation and awareness are essential cornerstones of suppleness. Suppleness is necessary for a horse to produce a good connection, impulsion, straightness, self-carriage, and good articulation of the limb joints.

Characteristics of Relaxation and Suppleness

When a horse is relaxed and supple in its work, the energy flow throughout its body becomes very fluid and the horse appears to be moving almost effortlessly. The rider's aids will be quickly recognized by the horse and the horse will willingly obey without resistance. This is known as throughness. When the horse is through, its back will be slightly up under the seat of the rider so that the rider can sit comfortably and, at the same time, the back can easily fulfill its role as a strong and supple bridge between the hindquarters and the forehand. The horse will also lengthen and lower its neck to some degree to create a connection to the bit. These characteristics are then reflected by a relaxed and swinging tail and a closed mouth on the horse. The mouth of the horse will remain closed without undue restraint from a nose band because the horse will be readily accepting contact with the bit and will have found self-carriage (Fig. 27).

When the horse is through, transitions can become almost effortless because the horse is well balanced, in self-carriage, and accepting the aids of the rider. Movements can become more precise for the same reason.

Traits of Good Relaxation and Suppleness

- **Fluid gaits**
- **Closed mouth with correct head carriage**
- **Effortless transitions**
- **Acceptance of rider aids**
- **Relaxed, swinging tail**
- **Precision of movements**
- **Straight - even on curved lines**

Fig. 27

Creating Mental Relaxation

Horses, like people, have difficulty learning if they are distracted, frightened or in pain. Hence, it is important for a rider to not only gain the trust as well as the respect of the horse, but also to acclimate the horse to its environment and introduce it to new places, sights, and activities. Ideally, this should start by imprinting when the foal is born. Horses are herd animals and foals that are allowed to interact with each other learn how to behave socially. Allowing youngsters to interact with older and more experienced horses, such as brood mares or barren mares, is also a good way of allowing them to learn from each other. Horses that are calm will have a calming effect upon youngsters who might be frightened. In addition, horses that have learned to interact successfully within a herd are less fearful later in life when they are ridden around other horses.

Working with the horse both from the ground as well as under saddle can help to instill trust, confidence, and respect in the horse.

A trainer should first learn to control his/her own emotions so that he/she can communicate with a horse in a calm and clear manner. Rewarding a horse for good behavior will reinforce that behavior but punishing it for unwanted behavior will not teach it to avoid that undesirable behavior.

Horses have long memories, but they live very much in the "now." Learned behaviors are never forgotten and will resurface whenever the circumstances that created them arise. At the same time, horses are mirrors of their riders and they will reflect both wanted and unwanted behaviors according to how they are being ridden as well as through their remembrances of similar circumstances. Horses will respond to the immediate aids of a rider, but their interpretation of the aids will also be based upon their remembrances. Horses are not mind readers and riders should learn how to communicate with them in the language of the horse. (See *Harmonic Dressage, Part 1, Optimizing Your Seat and Use of the Aids*.) Just because a horse may have exhibited some particular behavior in the past does not mean that the same behavior will be displayed under a *new set of circumstances*. If a horse is taught just one thing at a time and it is repeated three to five times in three to five different places, that behavior will start to become a generalization to the horse.

Creating Muscular Relaxation (Suppling)

Muscular relaxation or suppling is achieved primarily through bending exercises as well as exercises that make the horse cross its hind legs, such as turn on the forehand and leg-yield.

As previously mentioned, a horse can bend both laterally and longitudinally. Bending laterally, while at the same time also ensuring that the horse is stretching its neck down to seek contact with the hand of the rider, will help to supple the horse laterally (Fig. 28a). Framing the horse with the outside sides will then straighten the horse and create more longitudinal suppling (Fig. 28b)

> **Fig. 28** Suppling and Framing

Aston Kingsley Photo
Courtesy of Tami Thompson

Aston Kingsley Photo
Courtesy of Tami Thompson

Fig. 28a Lateral Suppling on a curved line

Fig. 28b Longitudinal Suppling and Framing on a Straight Line

The Anatomy of Bending

Bending exercises are essential tools for suppling a horse. However, how a horse bends its body has been a matter of discussion for many years and has led to some confusion in the minds of riders. The Federation Equestre Internationale (FEI) Rule Book states that when a horse bends, for example when circling, the body of the horse should adjust to the curvature of the line it follows (Fig. 29). In other words, the spine of the horse bends according to the arch of the curved line. This implies that a horse can bend its thoracic spine, which is where a rider is seated, like the shape of a "C." Although there is some lateral flexibility in the rib cage, there is almost no lateral flexibility between the thoracic vertebrae. Consequently, there is no spinal bending in the thoracic vertebrae on a curved line. However, there can be some movement through the soft tissue in the rib cage.

Fig. 29
Bending on a Circle as Shown in the F.E.I. Rule Book

If a rider bends a horse on a circle and attempts to create bend throughout the trunk of the horse by pulling on the inside rein and pushing sideways with his/her inside leg, he/she may displace the rib cage slightly laterally, but that will fail to turn the shoulders onto the arc of the circle. Instead, the horse will become hollowed on the inside with the haunches moving toward the inside of the circle and the shoulders pushing toward the outside of the circle.

To bend a horse so that the entire outside of the horse's body in on the circumference of a circle, a rider must create rotation in the sacroiliac and lumbosacral joints where the lower back and pelvis are joined. To do that, a rider creates rotation in the sacroiliac area by moving the hindquarters of the horse with his/her pelvis. By turning his/her upper body slightly (while keeping even weight on both sit bones) so that his/her inside shoulder and inside hip move slightly backwards towards the inside hip of the horse, a rider can move the pelvis of the horse to create engagement of the inside hind leg. At the same time, the rider must prevent the hindquarters and outside shoulder of the horse from swinging to the outside of the circumference of the circle with his/her outside leg and rein. The horse will then move its inside hind leg more underneath its belly, the hindquarters will engage, and the forehand of the horse will turn more towards the inside of the circle. In other words, the horse's body will be uniformly bent according to the circumference of the circle, and the hind feet will be the same tracks as the forefeet.

For a horse to bend on a curved line, both spinal and soft tissue components must be coordinated. Lateral and longitudinal bending can occur at just three places along the spine. The first place is between the axis and atlas, which is the joint where the head of the horse is joined to the backbone as shown in Fig. 30.

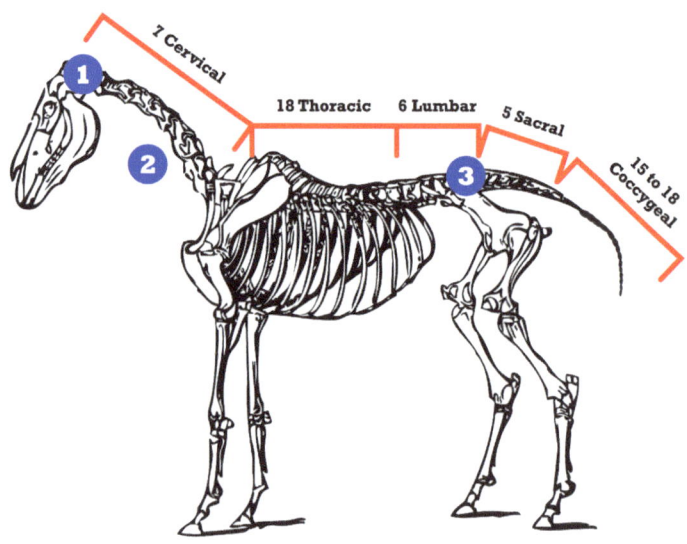

Fig. 30 Skeleton with Areas that Can Bend
1 Atlas and Axis Joint at the Poll
2 Cervical Vertebrae
3 Lumbosacral/Sacroiliac Joint

The second place is within the cervical (neck) vertebrae. The third place is in the sacroiliac and lumbosacral joint where the lower back joins the pelvis. The thoracic (chest) vertebrae that a rider sits upon as well as the lumbar (lower back) vertebrae do not bend laterally.

Lateral and longitudinal rotation must first be created in the lumbosacral (loin) area. As a horse bends in that area, the bend causes the inside hind leg of the horse to engage and step more underneath the belly of the horse. This then moves the thoracic and lumbar vertebrae (back) of the horse to the inside of a circle so that the shoulders of the horse are turned onto the circumference of the circle. The neck stays centered between the shoulder blades of the horse and simply follows a natural curvature. The rib cage of the horse will be slightly bent.

If a rider focuses upon keeping the backbone of the horse centered between his/her two sit bones (ischial tuberosity), the soft tissue of the horse together with the lateral bend produced as described above will fulfill the requirements of a horse's back bone appearing to be bent uniformly on a curved line (Fig. 31). The rider may not feel a lot of bend because most of it will be behind the saddle. The hind feet of the horse will be in alignment with the front feet. (Left hind footprint in the same track with the left front foot and right hind footprint in same track as right front foot.) Refer to *Harmonic Dressage Part 1, Optimizing Your Seat and Use of the Aids*, for further details.

Circling Right

Beginning Circle

Coming Out of Circle

Fig. 31 Circle to the Right with Correct Bend
Photos Courtesy of Christian Simonson riding Zeaball Diawind

Exercises to Promote Relaxation and Suppleness

Exercises In Hand That Help to Supple and Relax a Horse

- **Round Pen and Other Mental Conditioning Exercises**

    There are a multitude of excellent exercises that can be done at liberty in a round pen that can help to gain the trust and respect of a horse. In general, the trainer should direct the direction, but not necessarily the gait, in which the horse moves. By standing in the center of the round pen with a lunge whip, a trainer can move a horse either to the left or to the right by changing the hand in which they are holding the whip and moving towards the hindquarters of the horse, if necessary, to make it move in one direction or the other. The trainer can also make the horse turn to either the outside or the inside of the round pen when changing the direction of movement. By controlling the movement of the horse, the trainer exerts him/herself as the herd leader. When the exercise is stopped, the horse will also stop and come towards the trainer. At this point the trainer can move next to the horse and begin to walk. The horse will follow since it accepts the trainer as the leader.

A few trainers who have published books and or videos that I would recommend on this subject are, in alphabetical order: John Lyons, Robert Miller, D.V.M., Pat Parelli and Monty Roberts.

- ## Lungeing

Lungeing a horse gives a horse the chance to move its body freely while also learning to move forward. Lungeing can be done with or without tack, depending upon the goal of the trainer. It can also be done at liberty in an enclosed area to allow the horse more freedom of movement. Regardless of which way lungeing is done, it is important that the horse learns to pay attention to the trainer and move immediately forward from driving aids such as the voice or the flick of a lunge whip. When lungeing on a line, it is important that the horse pushes itself forward with energy and not just move the legs in a lazy fashion.

- ## Long Reining

Long reining (Fig. 321) is an art and science unto itself, and there are several ways that it can be done, depending on up the level of training of a horse as well as the knowledge and experience of a trainer. Done correctly, it is an extremely effective method that can be used to supple, connect, straighten, and collect a horse, but it is beyond the scope of this book to discuss in detail.

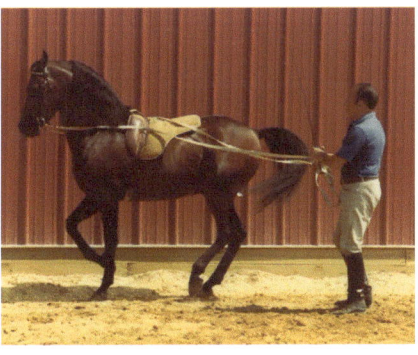

Fig. 32 Maj Hector Carmona Long Reins Serr Maariner

- **Unilateral and Diagonal Aids**

  The unilateral aids help to supple a horse and could be equated to the letter "A" in the alphabet because the alphabet must be learned before a word or sentence is formed. Likewise, a horse should first be suppled, "A," before framing, "B." Unilateral aids mean applying pressure to the bit and to the hind leg on the same side of the horse at the same time. They have the effect of getting a horse to stretch its neck down and follow its nose by turning the hindquarters and crossing the hind legs for one or two steps. In other words, the imaginary letter "A" teaches the horse that when pressure is applied to a rein, the horse should respond by seeking contact with the bit and engaging the hind leg on the same side.

The diagonal aids, can be equated to the letter, "B," in the alphabet. After a horse has learned to stretch its neck down and move its hindquarters, the diagonal aids are used to connect the inside hind leg of the horse with the outside rein. The diagonal aids (inside hind leg connected to the outside rein) are used to straighten and frame a horse while the unilateral aids help to first supple the horse laterally.

Since suppling is lower on the Training Pyramid than straightening, these exercises should be done in that order. The inside aids will create more suppleness, while the outside aids are applied to straighten and balance the horse.

- ### Unilateral Aids In-Hand
To teach a horse the unilateral aids in-hand, the trainer should stand near the head of the horse but face backwards towards the hindquarters. The trainer should then first hold the rein on the bit closest to him/her without putting any pressure on the bit. With a dressage whip, the trainer gently taps the upper hind leg of the horse on the same side to encourage the horse to step slightly forward. When the horse moves slightly forward, it will take contact with the bit and the hand of the trainer should simply resist against that pressure without pulling backwards. By continuing to encourage the horse to move forward and put pressure against the bit, the horse will

learn to round its back, relax its jaw, and stretch its neck down (Fig. 33a). As soon as the horse relaxes its jaw and stretches the neck down, the trainer should also immediately relax pressure on the bit so that the horse can straighten its neck. When unilateral aids are applied, the horse will first learn to do a turn on the forehand. The horse will also learn that when pressure is applied to the bit on one side that it should move its hind leg on the same side up and under its belly. This simple technique will help to supple a horse over its back as well as to teach the horse to relax its lower jaw and stretch its neck down to seek contact with the bit. Once the horse learns to relax on the inside jaw and step up to the bit, the horse can then be straightened and framed by using the diagonal aids (outside rein, Fig. 33b).

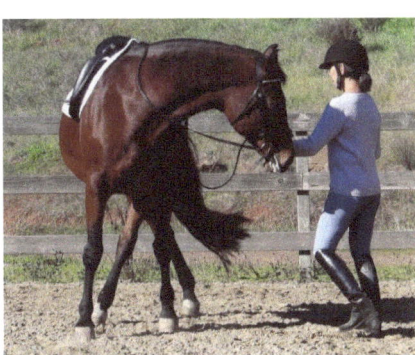

Photo Courtesy of Lorraine Kainuma

Fig. 33a
Horse Learning Unilateral Aids
The trainer has contact with only the INSIDE rein and asks horse to step up to the bit to yield in the jaw, stretch neck down and cross hind legs.

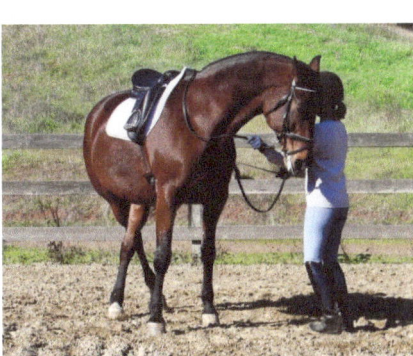

Photo Courtesy of Lorraine Kainuma

Fig. 33b **Horse Learning to Straighten into Diagonal Aids**
The trainer has contact with only the OUTSIDE rein and asks horse to step up to the bit, yield in the jaw, straighten neck, and cross hind legs.

Straightening will produce a better connection over the back of the horse provided that the trainer insists upon an active walk so that the horse yields in the jaw but also puts some positive pressure on the hand of the trainer to round its back. There are two ways a trainer can have contact with the outside rein (Fig. 33c). In one case the trainer simply places his/her arm under the neck of the horse and holds the outside rein. Another way is to pass the outside rein over the neck of the horse.

Fig. 33c **Two Horses Correctly Connected and Straightened Using Alternate Hand Positions**
Horses actively walking up and into the outside rein so that the back is rounded and the horse yields in the jaw but also puts some positive pressure on the rein.

Photo Courtesy of Lorraine Kainuma

Trainer Passes Arm Under Neck of Horse to take Contact with Outside Rein.

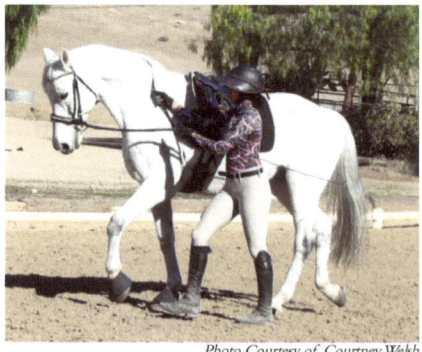

Photo Courtesy of Courtney Welsh

Trainer Passes Outside Rein Over the Neck of Horse

- **Common In-Hand Mistakes**
  Working a horse in-hand requires that a trainer learns to "read" the horse and coordinate his/her body language with the aids. Some common mistakes made by trainers learning to work horses in hand include getting ahead of the horse (Fig. 34a), letting the horse get ahead of the trainer (Fig. 34b), and allowing to horse to walk in a lazy fashion without pushing itself up to the bit (Fig. 34c). Compare these figures to Fig. 33c in which the horses are marching forward into light contact.

- **Solutions to the Mistakes**
  To prevent getting ahead of the horse, the trainer should wait for the horse to take light contact with the bit and begin to walk before the trainer walks.

  To prevent the horse from getting ahead of the trainer, the trainer must resist against the horse until the horse relaxes the lower jaw and walks forward with energy into light contact.

  To prevent horse from getting behind the driving aids, the trainer should encourage forward movement with the use of a whip and/or voice.

Fig. 34 Common Mistakes
Compare these Incorrect Figures to Correct Fig. 32c

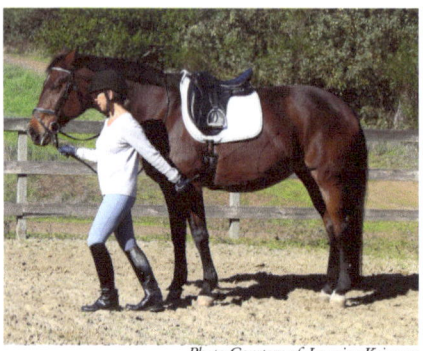
Photo Courtesy of Lorraine Kainuma

Photo Courtesy of Lorraine Kainuma

Fig. 34a Trainer Getting Ahead of the Horse (Incorrect)
Trainer with hand forward, losing contact with mouth of horse and walking before horse moves up to the bit.

Fig. 34b Horse Getting Ahead of the Trainer (Incorrect)
Horse actively walking, but the trainer is allowing the horse to put too much pressure on the outside rein without yielding in the jaw. Horse and rider are braced against each other.

Photo Courtesy of Lorraine Kainuma

Fig. 34c Horse Behind the Driving Aids (Incorrect)
Horse has walked up to the outside rein and yielded in the jaw. However, the trainer is allowing the horse to lose activity in the walk so the horse gets onto a more horizonal balance. Compare with Fig. 31c where the horse is moving forward in an "uphill" balance.

- **The Unilateral Aids Under Saddle**
  When the horse is circling, for example to the left, the rider flexes the horse to the left by raising the inside hand up and towards his/her outside shoulder, without crossing the hand over the withers. At the same time, the rider turns his/her upper body a little to the left (without lifting either sit bone) and applies some pressure with his/her left leg just behind the girth. Pressure is applied until the horse crosses its hind leg up and in front of the right hind leg and the horse turns sharply to the left. As soon as the horse responds by turning sharply to the left, the rider must immediately release pressure on the rein and allow the horse to straighten its neck. This is repeated until the horse becomes very laterally supple and sensitive to the aids (Fig. 35a-d).

The unilateral aids can be helpful for riders to check whether or not their horse is truly suppled on first one side and then the other. When the horse is suppled, it will stretch its neck down to seek contact with the bit and if the rider simply follows the connection as the horse stretches the rein downward and outward, the horse will become very pliable and relaxed while also engaging its inside hind leg and bending on the circle.

Fig. 35 Unilateral Aids Under Saddle to Supple on a Circle to the Left

Photo Courtesy of Sarah Borrey

Photo Courtesy of Sarah Borrey

Fig. 35a Unilateral Aids on Circle, Step 1
The rider picks up the left rein and waits for the horse to cross the left hind leg up and in front of the right hind, relax the lower jaw and stretch the neck down. The outside rein passively receives contact and prevents the horse from overbending its neck and pushing the outside shoulder to the outside of the circle.

Fig. 35b Unilateral Aids on Circle, Step 2
The rider releases pressure on the rein and allows the horse to turn in on the circle with the neck centered between the shoulder blades.

Photo Courtesy of Sarah Borrey

Photo Courtesy of Sarah Borrey

Fig. 35c Unilateral Aids on Circle, Step 3
The rider again puts pressure on the inside rein and turns her pelvis slightly to the left in order to turn the horse's pelvis so that the horse crosses the hind legs and turns the shoulders left into the circle.

Fig. 35d Unilateral Aids on Circle Step 4
The rider releases pressure on the inside rein and allows the horse to continue on the circle.

- ### The Diagonal Aids

Although the unilateral aids are very useful, if they are used exclusively, they tend to push the outside of the horse's body a little to the outside of the circle. This is true especially if the rider does not receive contact in the outside rein to prevent the horse from overbending its neck or fails to release the inside rein quickly enough once the horse is bent to allow the horse to straighten its neck. This problem is easily solved, however, by applying the diagonal outside rein to prevent the horse from overbending its neck to the inside. The diagonal rein pressure will then help to straighten and frame the horse.

When working with the unilateral aids, the role of the outside rein is to prevent the horse from overbending its neck to the inside so that the horse must step up and under its belly with the inside hind leg, engage the hindquarters, and bend its body. When the unilateral aids are applied, the diagonal aids can then also limit how far down and out the horse should stretch its neck in an effort to seek contact with the bit. The role of the outside leg is to prevent the horse from swinging its hindquarters sideways. By using the unilateral aids followed by the diagonal aids, the horse will first be suppled and relaxed by the unilateral aids. The horse will then be engaged, straightened, connected, and balanced more by the diagonal aids.

Exercises Under Saddle

- ### Traveling on Bending Lines
  Bending lines help to supple a horse by encouraging lateral flexibility followed by straightening. When changing the bend, a horse should first be straightened. Frequent changes of bend will help to bilaterally supple the horse. Remember that straightness means that the hind legs are in the same alignment as the tracks made by the front legs on both straight and curved lines. (Refer to Anatomy of Bending above.) Bending lines can include circles, serpentines, and figures of 8 of varying sizes (Fig. 36a-c).

Fig. 36 Bending Lines

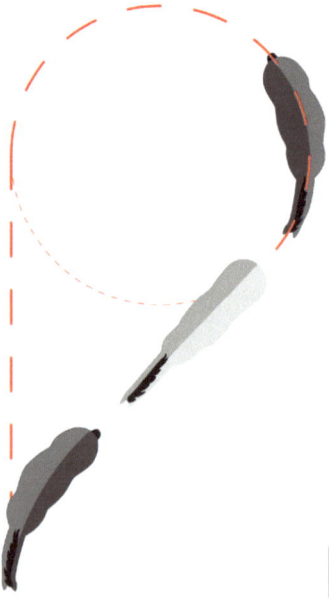

Fig. 36a
Circle and Half Cirle

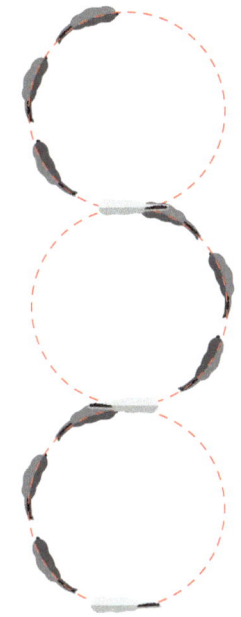

Fig. 36b Serpentine

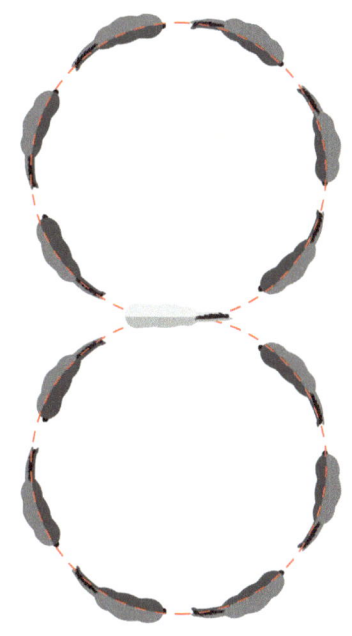

Fig. 36c Figure Eight

- **Turn on the Forehand**

  Turn on the forehand (Fig. 37) is an excellent exercise to first supple and loosen a horse by creating flexion opposite to the direction of movement and then straightening the horse by connecting to the outside aids. In turn on the forehand, the horse is flexed opposite to the direction of movement and the inside hindleg steps up and in front of the outside hind leg so that the horse moves its hindquarters around the front legs. Turn on the forehand can be 180° or 360°. The aids that the rider applies are like those used to do a leg-yield and thus can prepare a horse to do leg-yields.

Fig. 37 Turn on Forehand Left – Haunches Move to the Right
Photos Courtesy of Lorraine Kainuma

1

2

3

4

- **Leg-Yield**

    Leg yields (Fig. 38) require the horse to cross its legs as it moves forward and sideways while keeping its body straight. The horse will be flexed slightly at the poll opposite to the direction of movement and will move both forward and sideways. Leg-yields encourage freedom of movement, suppleness, looseness, regularity, and elasticity in the gaits.

    Leg-yields can also be done on bending lines as well as straight lines (Fig. 39). For instance, when leg-yielding on a circle, rather than bending on the circumference of the circle, the horse will cross its legs so that the hindquarters are either on the inside or the outside of the circle (Figs. 39a and 39b).

    Another variation of leg-yielding is to leg-yield with the horse facing either towards or away from a wall and on about a 35° angle to it (Fig. 39c). Leg-yields performed as a counter change of hand (leg-yield in one direction, straighten, change the flexion, and leg-yield in the opposite direction) or a zig zag (at least three changes of direction) help to create more equal suppling bilaterally.

Fig. 38 Leg-Yield to the Right

Fig. 39 Leg-Yield Variations

Photo Courtesy of Alberto Conde

Fig. 39a Leg-yield Left on Circle to the Left Puts Hindquarters on Inside of the Circle

Photo Courtesy of Alberto Conde

Fig. 39b Leg-Yield Right on a Circle to the Left Puts Hindquarters on Outside of the Circle

Photo Courtesy of Alberto Conde

Fig. 39c Leg-Yield with Head to the Wall

3. Contact and Connection
(Anlehnung)

For a horse to round its back and create a strong bridge between the hind quarters and the forehand, contact with the bit must be established. The horse must first be put well in front of the driving aids so that framing occurs when the horse obeys the activating aids of the seat and legs of the rider together with receiving aids of hands. This is known as the half-halt (Fig. 40). The seat and legs create a channel through which the horse is allowed to go forward to the contact. The hands *passively receive* the contact. Riders who take contact by pulling on the reins create tension and stiffness in the back of the horse. Good contact and framing are reflected in the elasticity of the connection, straightness and self-carriage of the horse.

A rider's correct position and use of the aids are paramount when creating a good connection over the back of the horse. A rider who does not sit correctly, use the aids correctly, or does not really *listen through his/her body* to what the horse is trying to communicate, will have a very difficult time creating a good connection over the back of the horse. See *Harmonic Dressage, Part 1, Optimizing Your Seat and Use of the Aids*, pages 38 and 39.

Half-Halt Mechanics

1. Rider breathes in and stretches body upward
2. Seat and leg press horse forward to the bit
3. Rider's lower back swings more slowly than horse's
4. Rider's hands receive forward motion
5. Rider breathes out and relaxes contact

Fig. 40 Mechanics of the Half-Halt in Trot

Creating and Assessing Contact and Connection

As a judge and clinician, it is my opinion that a good connection is one of the biggest challenges on the Training Pyramid for riders to conquer. More inexperienced riders sometimes think that contact is something they need to create by putting some amount of pressure on the reins with their own hands. Because of this, I prefer the word connection rather than contact because it stresses the use of the back of the horse rather than placing focus upon how much pressure is on the reins. Pressure on the reins is something that can and will change according to the skill of the rider as well as the balance and forwardness of the horse.

A horse moving in balance and with impulsion puts very light positive pressure on both reins with confidence. The amount of tension on the reins is determined by the horse, not by the rider, and must be a result of sufficient drive and thrust generated from the hindquarters. It should not be because of a rider tensing the muscles in his/her arms or pulling back on the reins. Although a horse might create considerable pressure on the reins during a half-halt, that amount of pressure will be only momentary.

To achieve good contact and framing, the horse must learn to stretch both reins down with confidence as it seeks contact with the bit. This is especially noticeable in upward transitions when the horse should try to lower its neck slightly and round its back more as it becomes more active in the hind legs. Once the upward transition has been established with a good connection, the back of the horse will be slightly rounded and the muscles on the back will contract and relax rhythmically in accordance with the gait of the horse. (Fig. 41) A rider will be able to feel through his/her seat whether the back of the horse is rounded and relaxed (connected) or hollow and stiff (disconnected).

Framing = Getting on the Aids

- **Horse obeys**
    1. Activating aids of rider's seat and legs
    2. Receiving aids of rider's hands

- **Physical = Muscular Relaxation**
    1. Horse raises withers and neck
    2. Horse finds resistance from the bit
    3. Horse yields in the jaw and at poll to achieve correct head position and round its back
    4. Rider pushes horse forward and relaxes arms a little, allowing horse to put positive pressure on the bit to promote self carriage and a positive connection.

Fig. 41

Contact and connection can be ever-changing based upon the frequency and effectiveness of the rider's half-halts as well as the balance, throughness, and self-carriage of the horse. Good balance and self-carriage are created primarily by a rider who can engage his/her core and create half-halts frequently and effectively. Half-halts are the mechanism whereby a rider rebalances a horse. They are the moment when a rider speaks nonverbally to the horse. After the half-halt, the rider should relax and listen by feeling the response of the horse. A rider's use of aids to perform half-halts effectively is detailed in *Harmonic Dressage, Part 1, Optimizing Your Seat and Use of the Aids*.

Mounted Exercises to Enhance Suppleness and Connection

- ### Framing using Unilateral Followed by Diagonal Aids

  As mentioned previously, the unilateral aids followed by use of the diagonal aids will first supple a horse and then frame and straighten it. The unilateral inside aids teach the horse that when pressure is applied to the inside rein, the horse should move its inside hind leg up and under its belly and stretch its neck down to seek contact with the bit. However, it is easy for a horse to stretch its neck downward and sideways too much and get onto the forehand. The rider should limit the degree of lateral bend through the neck with the outside rein. This prevents the horse from pushing the shoulders to the outside. The outside leg of the rider should prevent the hindquarters from pushing to the outside. In this way, the horse will begin to straighten and to establish a better connection over its back together with good balance and self-carriage (Fig. 42).

Fig. 42 Lateral Suppling Followed by Framing and Straightening

Photo Courtesy of Karin Harkin

Fig. 42a
Horse suppled with unilateral aids

Photo Courtesy of Judi Devore

Fig. 42b
Horse framed and straightened with diagonal aids

- ### Effects of framing

  Correct contact and framing together with necessary impulsion (Fig. 43) will result in the back of horse becoming soft and swinging. In addition, the poll of the horse will become highest point of whole horse with the nose slightly ahead of, or on, the vertical line, depending upon the degree of collection. The ears of the horse should stay on the same level (head not tipping or tilting sideways.) With correct contact and connection, the horse will find self-carriage and the gaits will become more fluid.

Photo Courtesy of Katarina Antens Miller

Fig. 43 **Correct Contact and Connection**
Straight Line from Elbow to Mouth of Horse. The poll is the highest point of neck with the nose slightly in front of vertical, mouth closed and back of horse forming a strong bridge between hindquarters and forehand. This creates engagement of hindquarters and relative lifting of the forehand.

- **Incorrect Contact and Connection**

  If the horse's neck is bent by the hand of the rider so that the horse's neck becomes bent at the third cervical vertebra, the horse will come behind the bit and the reins will become loose. When the rider also fails to push the horse forward, the gaits of the horse will become flatter, and the horse will fail to put any positive pressure on the bit (Fig. 44).

Fig. 44 Horse Behind the Bit and Bent at Third Cervical Vertebra

If a rider fails to get the horse to stretch its neck down and seek contact with the bit, the back of the horse will become hollow. The gaits of the horse will become shorter and less elastic because the back of the horse is no longer creating a good bridge between the hindquarters and forehand. (Fig. 45) A horse with a hollow back can neither go forward well nor engage the hindquarters.

Fig. 45 Horse Above the Bit with Back Hollowed

- **Transitions Enhance Connection**
Transitions, transitions, and more transitions between gaits and between the paces within each gait are key to creating good communication between horse and rider. They also serve to create a better connection over the back of the horse. Begin with walk-halt-walk transitions until the horse can remain connected and in contact with the bit in both upward and downward transitions. This will help to tune the horse to the aids of the rider and show the rider how responsive the horse is to the aids. Halts followed by rein backs will increase the sensitivity of the horse to the aids of the rider and create more throughness. It is very important for a rider to realize that a horse must stay in front of the driving aids of the rider. A rider should be able to put very light leg pressure on the rib cage of the horse and have the horse respond almost immediately. Riders who are continuously heavy with their aids simply make the horse dead to the aids so that both horse and rider end up having to work inefficiently and with much greater effort.

- **Traits of Good Contact and Connection**
When good contact and framing are achieved, the back of the horse will become slightly arched or rounded and it will swing easily according to

the gait it is in. The poll of the horse will become the highest point of its neck and the neck will be stretched so that the nose of the horse is slightly in front of an imaginary vertical line to the ground or on the vertical. The ears of the horse will be level, indicating that the head is not tilted or tipping. The mouth of the horse will be closed, indicating that the horse is in self carriage (See Fig. 43 and Fig. 46).

Correct Contact and Framing

- Horse's back soft and swinging
- Poll is highest point
- Nose slight ahead - or on - vertical
- Ears level - head not tipping
- Mouth closed

Fig. 46

4. Impulsion *(Schwung)*

Impulsion is the willingness to move forward with energy. It is dependent upon the horse having rhythmic and regular gaits (**Element 1**) as well as a supple and strong back created through a good connection (**Elements 2 and 3**). Figures 47a and 47b illustrate the effect of impulsion after a horse is first suppled and connected.

When good impulsion is achieved, the gaits of the horse will show elasticity, increased suspension in the trot and canter, and good articulation of the joints (Fig. 47b). The hindquarters will become well engaged, and the steps of the horse will become more ground-covering. The horse will track up more from behind so that the hind feet land in front of the hoof prints of the front feet in the walk and trot and there is clear separation of the hind legs in the canter. Since impulsion is not about speed, a consistent tempo will occur between the paces within a gait. The rider will feel the horse's back relaxed and swinging as the horse carries the rider forward and the gaits become energetic and expressive.

Fig. 47 Impulsion Creates Better Connection, Straightness, and Engagement

Photo Courtesy of Efrain Guzman

Photo Courtesy of Katarina Antens Miller

Fig. 47a Horse stretches neck down and out to take contact with the bit in order to round the back

Fig. 47b Adding More Impulsion creates a better connection and uphill balance

Some riders think that to move forward they must move faster. However, when a horse moves forward, it needs to maintain balance and not rush onto the forehand. This creates more airtime in the moment of suspension as the result of thrust and the releasing of energy stored in the hind legs by engagement and active articulation of the joints in the hind limbs. When a rider develops impulsion, the gaits become loftier.

On the other hand, if a horse is made to move too rapidly, the moment of suspension is decreased, and the gaits become flatter. To visualize this, look at dressage horses doing extended trot or canter with big, unhurried steps compared to racehorses. (Fig. 48)

Fig. 48 Impulsion vs. Speed

Photo Courtesy of Tami Thompson

Jack Ledbetter   Photo Courtesy of Glenn Thompson

Fig. 48a
Impulsion showing a loftier and more cadenced canter than speed

Fig. 48b
Speed creates a flatter and faster canter

Impulsion does not apply to the walk, since there is no moment of suspension, i.e., a moment when all four feet are off the ground at the same time. However, walks can show greater or lesser activity and ground-covering steps. Because forwardness is associated with impulsion, it encompasses ground-covering steps as well as a clear, marked rhythm and tempo. Traits of good impulsion are shown in Fig. 49.

Traits of Good Impulsion

- Elastic gaits with clear suspension
- Hind quarters well engaged
- Ground covering steps
- Tracking up from behind
- Steady tempo between paces
- Swinging back
- Energetic, expressive movements

Fig. 49

- **Enemies of Impulsion**
Quick, hurried steps and irregularity are the enemies of impulsion. To achieve forwardness, one must shift the horse's center of gravity more backwards using half-halts. Imagine that a horse is like a seesaw. If there is equal weight front and back, your horse will be in a horizontal balance. If all the weight of the horse is shifted back, then the horse would be rearing and standing on his hind legs. On the other hand, if the center of gravity shifted too far forward, the horse would be kicking up behind and standing on its front legs. Shifting the center of gravity back so that the horse lifts the forehand and engages the hindquarters while moving forward with elasticity and expression is the goal of impulsion. This means that the rider must work with half-halts to move the center of gravity backward followed by forward, ground-covering movements. The horse is not only more engaged in his hind legs, but also pushes off more strongly with his hind legs (thrust). This sequence of a half-halt followed by moving forward needs to be repeated frequently and in rapid succession to help the horse lift the forehand, find uphill balance, develop impulsion, and remain forward.

Forwardness requires energy. There are two types of energy a horse can produce: potential energy and kinetic energy. Potential energy can be likened to a compressed spring that is ready to expand but is kept coiled tightly. Kinetic energy can be likened to when the spring is suddenly allowed to unfold and rapidly expand. Potential energy is stored energy that has the possibility to expand whereas kinetic energy is the energy of movement and produces speed and ground cover. A horse that is in good balance and is forward will have the right mix of potential and kinetic energy. Such a horse will be able to quickly either lengthen or shorten its steps without changing tempo (speed of the rhythm).

- **Achieving Balance**

To find balance is to find harmony, freedom of motion and expression without tension. Balance puts the horse into a zone of all possibilities where it can immediately perform any upward or downward transition almost effortlessly. To achieve good balance, the rider must have a good seat that allows the horse to find his own correct balance. If the rider leans too far forward and gets in front of the movement of the horse, the horse will likely try to quicken its steps to support the rider's weight. Likewise, if the rider leans too far back or sits too heavily, the horse will tense his back to support the weight and that, in turn, will then interfere with the horse's natural ability to move with freedom. Refer to *Harmonic Dressage, Part 1* for further discussion of the role of the rider.

5. Straightness *(Gerarderichtung)*

The second to highest element of the Training Pyramid is straightness. Straightness means that the hind feet are in alignment with the front feet on both straight and curved lines. However, since the hindquarters of the horse are broader than the forehand, they don't naturally come into that alignment (Fig. 50). Straightness is the key to collection, but it is also dependent upon the four lower elements. Straightness is achieved especially through engagement of the hindquarters together with impulsion.

- ### Achieving Straightness
  To straighten a horse so that the hind feet do come into alignment with the front feet, the horse must be taught to travel with its hind legs closer together. This is done through lateral movements such as shoulder-fore or shoulder-in. To do a lateral movement, it is necessary for the horse to engage its hindquarters which then allows the horse to move its hind legs closer together. Engagement allows the hind legs to travel in alignment with the same tracks as the front legs (Fig. 51).

Fig. 50
Natural Nonalignment of Hind Feet with Front Feet

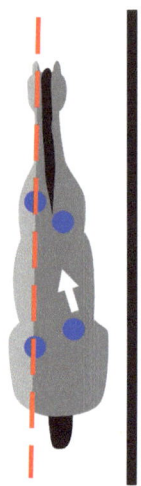

Fig. 51
Straightening a Horse with Shoulder-Fore

Lateral Exercises to Improve Straightness

Lateral movements done with sufficient impulsion (Element 4) enhance both suppleness (Element 2) and connection (Element 3). When the horse is then allowed to straighten, the hind legs can come into alignment with the front legs due to engagement of the hindquarters. However, when lateral movements are done with the horse on the forehand because of lack of impulsion, more crookedness and spreading of the hind legs can be created. When done with energetic impulsion, the lateral movements create both lateral and longitudinal bend together with more bend in the joints of the hind limbs. This increase in both lateral and longitudinal bend creates more straightness (Element 5) and collection (Element 6) due to suppled engagement of the hindquarters.

- Shoulder-in is the first of the lateral exercises designed to create more engagement of the hindquarters. Shoulder-in makes the horse bends both laterally and longitudinally. This bending makes the horse step more underneath its body with the inside hind leg so that the hind legs can travel closer together. In shoulder-in, the inside hind leg of the horse comes into the same track as the outside front leg (Fig. 52 and 53a). To then straighten a horse, the shoulders of the horse are brought back toward the track to create shoulder-fore (Fig. 53b). Unlike the shoulder-in, the shoulder-fore creates only flexion, but no bend through the body of the horse. In shoulder-fore, the inside hind leg of The horse travels between the front legs. When the horse is finally straightened, the hind legs come into alignment with the front legs (Fig. 53c). To be straightened, the horse must engage the hindquarters by bending longitudinally in the lumbo-sacral joint. Straightness is achieved first through lateral flexibility and then through engagement of the hindquarters created by the hind legs travelling closer together so that they can come into alignment with the front legs.

Specifics of Shoulder-In

- Key purpose: Teach horse to engage inside hind leg and move more narrowly via bending in loin
- Horse bent around inside leg of rider (near girth)
- Inside hind leg in same track as outside foreleg
- Flexion of poll to inside
- Hind quarters parallel to the wall

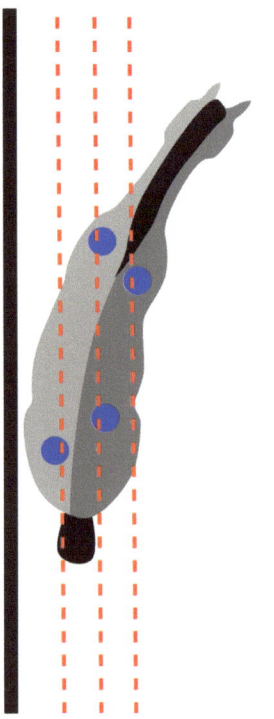
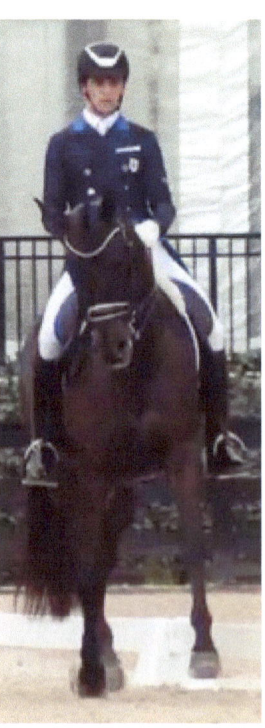

Photo Courtesy of Christian Simonson

Fig. 52

Fig. 53
Straightening a Horse Starting from Shoulder-In

Photo Courtesy of Christian Simonson

Author

Photo Courtesy of Sarah Graham

Fig. 53a
Shoulder-In creates both lateral and longitudinal bending with engagement of the hindquarters

Fig. 53b
Shoulder-Fore Creates flexion throughout the body of the horse, but not bend

Fig. 53c
When the shoulders are returned to the track, the horse is straightened through engagement of the hindquarters

- **Travers and Renvers** require more engagement of the hindquarters as well as more bend than shoulder-in. In travers and renvers, the horse is on four tracks but in shoulder-in, the horse is on three tracks (Figs. 54 and 55). Travers and renvers are the same type of bend but indicate whether the haunches are in (travers) or out (renvers) relative to the position of the wall (Fig. 55a and 55b). Likewise, shoulder-in (Fig. 55c) and shoulder-out are the same kind of bend and simply relate to the position of the wall.

Lateral Movements to Improve Straightness

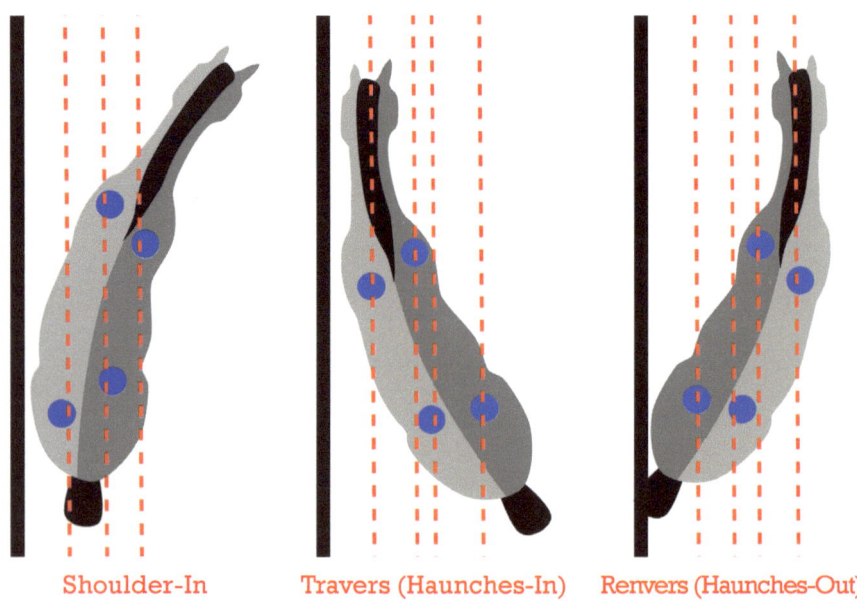

Shoulder-In   Travers (Haunches-In)   Renvers (Haunches-Out)

Fig. 54 Position of the Legs in Lateral Movements

Lateral movements help to increase both suppleness and engagement. The lateral movements, when intermixed with each other and used in succession, will help to create more bilateral (equal on left and right,) suppling and elastic collection.

Fig. 55
Comparison of Bend in Lateral Movements

Fig. 55a Travers (haunches-in) on four tracks

Fig. 55b Renvers (Haunches-out) is opposite of travers

Fig. 55c Shoulder-In on three tracks

In travers, the horse is bent in the direction of movement. The bend is primarily created in the lumbosacral and sacroiliac joints, increasing engagement of the hind quarters. Travers requires more bend and engagement of the hindquarters than shoulder-in. However, when riding a travers, the rider may not feel much bend because most of it is in the loin area behind the saddle. The outside shoulder and the center of the chest of the horse move straight ahead and parallel to the wall (Fig. 56). To straighten a horse from travers, the haunches are brought back to the track. When the outside hind leg of the horse steps up and between the two front legs, the horse is said to be "in position".

Specifics of Travers (Haunches-In)

- Key Purpose to increase collection
- Horse bent in direction of movement
- Flexion to inside
- Shoulders parallel to the wall
- Four tracks

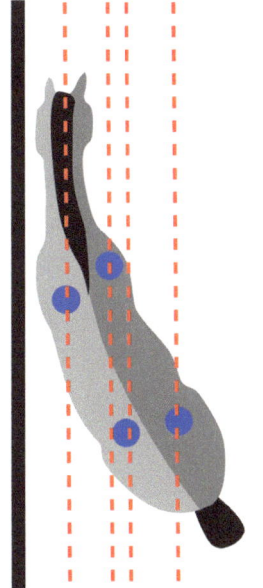  

Photo Courtesy of Mallory Schneider   *Photo Courtesy of Mallory Schneider*

Fig. 56

- **Half Pass,** another lateral movement, is a variation of travers. The half-pass will also enhance the collection of the horse by creating suppled engagement. Figs. 57 and 58 demonstrate how the half-pass is a variation of travers. A rider might imagine that the outside wall of the arena was simply displaced and put onto a diagonal line (Fig. 57). The half-pass is created by riding a travers next to the imaginary diagonal wall.

Half Pass = Tavers on a Diagonal Line

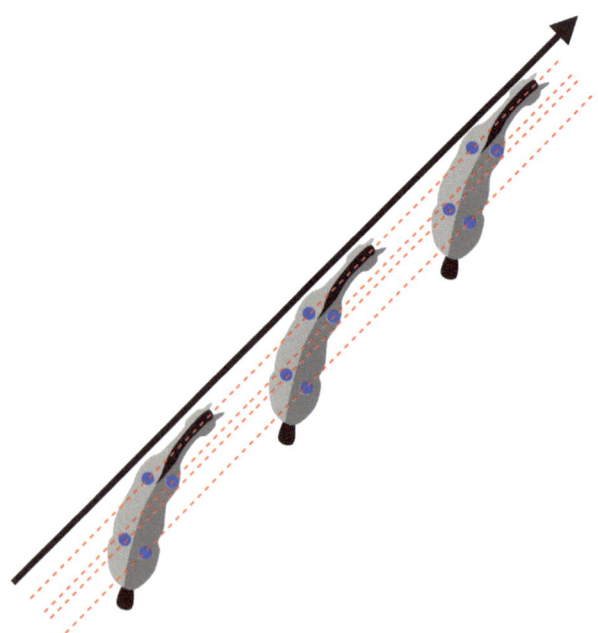

Fig. 57 Mechanics of Half-Pass
The Outside Shoulder and Center of Chest of Horse are Parallel to an Imaginary Diagonal Line

As the steepness of the half-pass increases, for instance, half-pass from "K" to "B" as opposed to a half-pass from "K" to "X", the bend of the travers must also increase (Fig 58). Because the horse has no lateral flexibility in the thoracic vertebrae, the horse cannot bend its body in the shape of a "C". Instead, bending occurs in the loin area behind the saddle as well as somewhat in the soft tissue of the rib cage. This additional bending creates engagement of the hindquarters and collection. In all the lateral movements, the neck of the horse should not be overbent. Instead, it should stay centered between the shoulder blades of the horse.

Photo Courtesy of Olympian Adrienne Lyle riding Wizard

Fig. 58 **Half-pass Right from "K" to "B"**
The Outside Shoulder and Center of Chest of Horse are Parallel to an Imaginary Diagonal Line.

6. Collection *(Versammlung)*

At the top of the Training Pyramid is collection. Collection is a result of all the elements of the Training Pyramid being put together in the right order. In other words, a rider should supple a horse through bending exercises followed by connection and contact with the bit. Once the horse is suppled and connected, it is then possible to create better impulsion, which then leads to straightness. Straightness then creates suppled collection. On the other hand, if a rider tries to ride a horse straight without first suppling it, that straightness will create a stiff-backed horse rather than a collected horse whose back is relaxed and swinging. All the elements interact with each other and are equally important, but the order in which they are introduced into the training of the horse is of paramount importance because each element creates a foundation for the higher elements, and they build upon each other.

Collection and the Training Pyramid

Adhering to the hierarchy of the Training Pyramid will train a horse to first become laterally supple and relaxed (Element 2). Next, contact and connection (Element 3) will frame the horse and, together with impulsion (Element 4) start to create straightness (Element 5). Suppled straightness is the key to good collection (Element 6) and all of the elements together will improve the gaits (Element 1) of the horse.

When a horse is collected, it should show pure and regular gaits (Element 1), suppleness and mental relaxation (Element 2), elastic connection (Element 3), expressive impulsion (Element 4), enhanced balance produced through straightness (Element 5), and engagement of the hindquarters which produces collection (Element 6). Comparing the training of a horse to the composition of music, one can visualize how suppled, obedient, elastic, and expressive collection in a horse is the result of all the elements or notes of the Training Pyramid being played first as a scale and then intermingled to create music.

It is important to note that simply shortening the steps of any gait does not create collection. Instead, the balance and equilibrium of the horse should be improved through suppled engagement of the hind quarters and a relative lifting of the forehand. The back of the horse should be supple and elastic as the horse becomes straighter and more collected.

High collection reflects the near perfect balance and self-carriage of the horse and is easily seen in canter pirouettes, piaffe, and passage (Figs. 59, 60, and 61).

Photo Courtesy of Olympian, Sabine Schut-Kery, and Anne Womble, owner of Sanceo

Photo Courtesy of Olympian, Adrienne Lyle, and Havensafe Farm, owner of Salvino

Fig. 59 **Canter Pirouette**

Photo of Courtesy of Jorge Gabriel riding Elmo Santana

Susan Stickle Photo Courtesy of Olympian, Sabine Schut-Kery, and Anne Womble, owner of Sanceo

Fig. 60 Piaffe

Photo of Courtesy of Jorge Gabriel riding Elmo Santana

Susan Stickle Photo Courtesy of Olympian, Adrienne Lyle, and Havensafe Farm, owner of Salvino

Fig. 61 Passage

The Movements and Their Purpose

Halt

The halt should be produced through a series of half-halts created by increased action of the seat and legs of the rider into a closed, but not pulling, hand. If the halt is performed abruptly, the benefits of this movement are lost.

Purpose
The halt shifts weight onto hindquarters, promoting engagement and connection.

Half - Halt

The half-halt is an almost simultaneous coordinated action of the seat and legs of the rider to press the horse up into the hands.

Purpose
Half-halts increase the attention of the horse and prepare it to execute a movement or transition. By shifting the weight of the horse more onto the hindquarters and increasing engagement, the horse is brought into better balance. Frequent half-halts improve the balance, lightness and responsiveness of the horse.

Rein Back

The rein back is a rearward movement with a diagonal, two beat rhythm. However, unlike the trot, there is no moment of suspension. The horse should remain on the bit with the poll the highest point of the neck, light in the hand, calm and straight. In addition, the horse should maintain its desire to move forward and, after the rein back, the horse should immediately move forward with a fluid and direct transition to the required gait.

Purpose
The rein back, especially when done in series, like a swing between rein backs with walk steps in between (Schaukel), promotes thoroughness and a better connection.

Transitions

Transitions between gaits, paces, or movements should be fluid and prompt but not abrupt. The horse should maintain its desire to move forward in both upward and downward transitions. The rhythm and tempo of the gait or pace should be maintained up until the transition is made to another movement, gait or halt. The horse should remain on the bit, light in the hand, calm and maintain its position (not, for instance, swinging the hindquarters during a transition.)

Purpose

Transitions promote responsiveness, throughness, and a better connection. In addition, the horse learns paces and movements more quickly through transitions than by simply maintaining a pace or movement.

Changes of Direction

In changes in direction, the horse should adjust the bend of its body to the curvature of the line it follows. The hind feet of the horse should be in alignment with the tracks of the front feet. When changing bend, the horse should be straightened before changing direction (Figs. 35a–c).

Figures that require a change of bend include serpentines, counter change of hand (half-pass in one direction followed by a half-pass in the opposite direction,) zig zag (more than two half-passes with change of direction,) and figures of eight (two connected circles of equal size.)

Purpose

Horses, like people, usually have a dominant side and a weaker side or a convex side and a hollow side. Frequent changes of direction help the horse to become more bilaterally supple.

Leg-Yield

The horse is flexed opposite to the direction of movement and then straightened with the outside leg and rein so that the body of the horse becomes straight with slight flexion only at the poll. The inside legs of the horse step up in front of and cross the outside legs as the horse moves both forward and sideways (See Fig. 38).

Purpose
To make the horse more sensitive to the aids of the rider and to create more suppleness and freedom of movement. Leg-yields can also improve the rhythm and regularity of the gaits.

Turn on the Forehand

The aids for turn on the forehand are like those used to create leg-yields. The horse is flexed slightly opposite to the direction of movement and the hindquarters are moved around the forehand (See Fig. 37).

Purpose
Similar to the leg-yield, turn on the forehand makes the horse more obedient to the aids and creates more suppleness and connection.

Shoulder - In and Shoulder - Fore

Shoulder-in occurs when the inside hind leg of the horse travels in alignment with the outside front leg and the shoulders of the horse are displaced to the inside track. Shoulder-in requires the horse to bend, engage the inside hind leg, and lower the haunches. It is the first of the lateral movements used to teach a horse to collect (See Fig. 52).

Shoulder-fore is achieved when the inside hind leg of the horse steps up and between the two front legs and the outside front and hind legs stay in alignment. (See Fig. 53b) Shoulder-fore requires engagement of the hind quarters and flexion, but not bend, through the body of the horse. Shoulder-in, followed by allowing the shoulders of the horse to return to the track, without allowing the hind quarters to push to the outside, can result in a shoulder-fore. Straightness is created from the shoulder-fore when the shoulders are brought parallel to the wall (See Fig. 53).

Purpose

Shoulder-fore and shoulder-in together with impulsion create better connection and straightness. These elements then serve as a bridge to the highest elements on the training-scale. Together with impulsion, shoulder-in creates engagement of the inside hind leg so that the hind legs travel closer together. Since the hindquarters are wider than the forehand, shoulder-in, followed by allowing the shoulders to return to the track in shoulder-fore, allows straightening of the horse. When a horse is straight, the hind quarters will be engaged, and the hind legs will travel in alignment with the respective front legs. Shoulder-in done without good impulsion or with the neck of the horse turned in so that the outside shoulder is pushed to the outside, has the opposite effect upon the horse by creating crookedness rather than engagement and straightness.

Travers, Renvers, Riding in Position and Half-Pass

These lateral movements differ from shoulder-in because they are done on four rather than three tracks (See Fig. 54) Half-pass is a variation of travers and requires more bend through the body of the horse as the steepness of the angle increases. For instance, half-pass from "K" to "X" requires less bend than half-pass from "K" to "B" (See Figs. 57 and 58).

Purpose
Together with good impulsion, all of the lateral movements increase the degree of suppleness, engagement and collection of the horse because they teach the horse to move the hind legs closer together. Lateral movements also improve the rhythm, regularity, and cadence of the gaits.

Just as shoulder-in followed by shoulder-fore and straightening work together, in a similar manner, travers, followed by riding "in position," also helps to increase the degree of suppleness, engagement, straightness, and collection of the horse.

Riding "in position" means that the outside hind leg of the horse steps up and between the two front legs while the inside front and hind legs stay in alignment (Fig. 62). It is the opposite of shoulder-fore where the inside hind leg steps up and between the two front legs. Flexion, but not bending, is created through the body of the horse in both shoulder-fore and riding "in position."

When shoulder-fore and riding "in position" are intermixed in succession, they create more bilateral suppling, a better connection over the back of the horse and, together with impulsion, they serve to promote straightness and collection.

Photo Courtesy of Sarah Graham

Fig. 62
Riding "in position"

Pirouette and Turn on the Haunches

The pirouette or half pirouette is a half-pass around the tip of the tail of the horse with the forehand moving around the haunches (Fig. 63). The pirouette is the length of the horse. Working pirouettes are larger, up to 3m, than pirouettes. Pirouettes can be performed at the walk, canter, and piaffe. Pirouettes require great engagement of the hindquarters and lightness of the forehand (See Fig. 59).

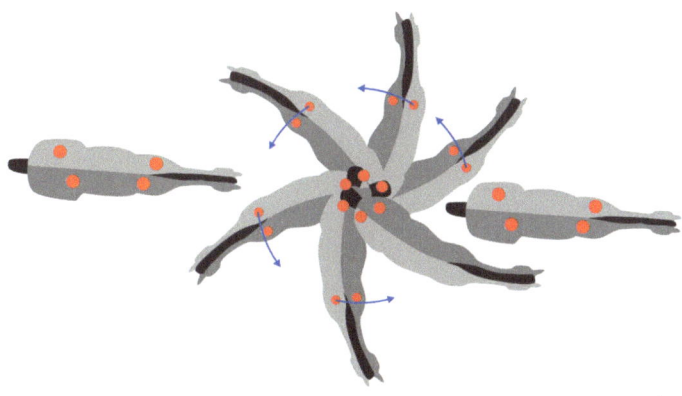

Fig. 63 **Pirouette**

Turn on the haunches is done at the walk and is like the pirouette but might be about 1m larger than the pirouette, which is just the length of the horse. Turn on the haunches is for younger horses that have not yet developed a collected walk. It is done out of the medium walk through a series of half-halts to shorten the steps of the walk.

Purpose
The turn on the haunches, working pirouette, and pirouette gradually increase the degree of collection of the walk or canter by shortening the steps of the gait while also increasing the activity of the hind legs. This creates more engagement of the hindquarters (collection).

Piaffe

Piaffe is very animated and is the highest degree of collection a horse can achieve. Giving the impression of trotting on the same spot, the piaffe is cadenced and elevated through lowering and engagement of the hindquarters together with increased bending and activity in the joints of the legs. (See Fig. 60). The horse should not swing the forehand or the hindquarters nor squat by spreading the hind legs. The back of the horse should remain supple and elastic.

Purpose
The piaffe creates the maximum degree of collection a horse can attain. It brings the horse into near perfect balance.

Passage

The passage is a highly collected trot (See Fig. 61). There is pronounced engagement of the hind quarters and the steps become shorter, more elevated, and very cadenced. In passage, the steps should be regular and neither the forehand nor the hindquarters should swing from side to side.

Purpose
The passage increases the degree of impulsion, straightness and collection of the horse.

Putting it All Together

The Training Pyramid is a clear and logical system for training any horse in any discipline. The first three elements of the Training Pyramid, rhythm and regularity, Element 1, relaxation and suppleness, Element 2, and contact and connection, Element 3, form the foundation of any training program. Impulsion, Element 4, is the bridge between the lower and higher elements. Straightness, Element 5, and collection, Element 6, apply more importantly to upper-level dressage work and disciplines that require more collection. However, it is important to keep in mind that all six elements interact with each other and profoundly affect each other.

The word, *dressage*, means training, and it is a progressive system that can culminate in high collection. Not all horses are capable of upper-level dressage nor is high collection necessarily the goal in many disciplines. Never-the-less, adhering to the Training Pyramid system will make any horse more supple, more responsive to the seat and aids of the rider, more relaxed mentally and physically, and will promote better health and soundness in the horse.

For example, the use of the Training Pyramid in flat work for jumpers will improve their ability to do their job by making them more balanced and responsive to riding between the fences. Although the goal of an upper-level jumper is different from an upper-level dressage horse, using the Training Pyramid to train jumpers helps to keep these horses sound, supple, more capable of shifting their weight onto the hind quarters, and, lengthen or shorten their strides to adjust to distances between fences. It will also enhance the rideability of these horses between fences.

Another example of the value of the Training Pyramid is its use in starting racehorses. Racehorses that are initially trained according to the principles of the Training Pyramid are more balanced, supple, and responsive to the aids. This makes them easier for jockeys to ride. Racing does not require high collection, which is the goal especially of the higher three elements of the Training Pyramid. However, a supple and well-connected horse, which is the focus of the first three elements of the Training Pyramid, will stay sounder and will be easier to ride.

Correct training of a horse requires that a rider first learns to sit on a horse correctly without interfering with its balance. A rider must then learn how to correctly use his/her body, arms and legs, together with the auxiliary aids, when necessary. These tools will allow a rider to communicate with the horse through body language so that horse and rider are able to achieve a running conversation as the horse is ridden.

Harmonic Dressage ® Manuals

Harmonic Dressage Part 1, Optimizing Your Seat and Use of the Aids, describes in detail how a rider can develop and maintain a running conversation with the horse.

Harmonic Dressage Part 2, Techniques of Harmonic Dressage and the Training Pyramid, outlines a specific protocol for training a horse. It also describes various movements commonly used to train a horse together with their purpose.

Harmonic Dressage Part 3, Methodology of Harmonic Dressage, sets forth specific techniques and methodology that can be used to train horses in keeping with the principles of the Training Pyramid.

Index

aids
    activating, 69
    diagonal, 39, 55, 56, 57, 63, 73
    driving, 69
    receiving, 69
    unilateral, 39 55, 56, 57, 62, 63, 73

    balance, 84
bend
    anatomy of, 47
    lateral, 13, 39, 46, 50, 51,
    longitudinal, 13, 39, 46, 50, 51

canter paces, 31
canter pirouettes, 98, 107
cavaletti, 40
collection, 96, 97
connection, 38, 58, 69, 70, 71, 72, 73, 75, 77, 78

dressage, 110

flat work, 110
framing, 39, 55, 71, 72, 74, 78

gaits
    deviations, 35, 36, 37
    elastic, 19, 79
    irregularity, 7, 40
    paces, 8
    purity, 8
    regularity, 22, 23, 24, 39,
    rhythm, 22, 23, 24, 39
    tempo, 22, 23, 24

half-halt, 69, 70, 100
half-pass, 94, 95, 105
halt, 49, 100

I

impulsion, 79, 81, 82
in position, 92, 106
in-hand, 56, 57, 58, 59, 60

J

jumpers, 111

K

kinetic energy, 83

L

leg-yield, 67, 68, 103
lungeing, 54

P

passage, 98, 99, 109
piaffe, 98, 99, 108
potential energy, 83

R

racehorses, 81, 111
rein back, 101
relaxation, 41, 42, 43, 44, 46
renvers, 90, 91, 105
round pen, 53

S

Shoulder-fore, 85, 86, 89
shoulder-in, 85, 87, 88, 89
shoulder-out, 90
stiffness, 19, 38, 69
straightness, 85, 89
suppleness, 35, 42, 43, 44, 46

T

throughness, 43
training pyramid
    hierarchy, 10, 11, 13, 96
Training Scale, 16
Training Wheel, 16, 17
transitions, 77, 101
travers, 90, 91, 92, 105
trot paces, 27, 28, 29, 30
turn on the forehand, 66, 103
turn on the haunches, 107

W

walk paces, 25, 26

www.ingramcontent.com/pod-product-compliance
Lightning Source LLC
Chambersburg PA
CBHW041216070526
44583CB00001B/5